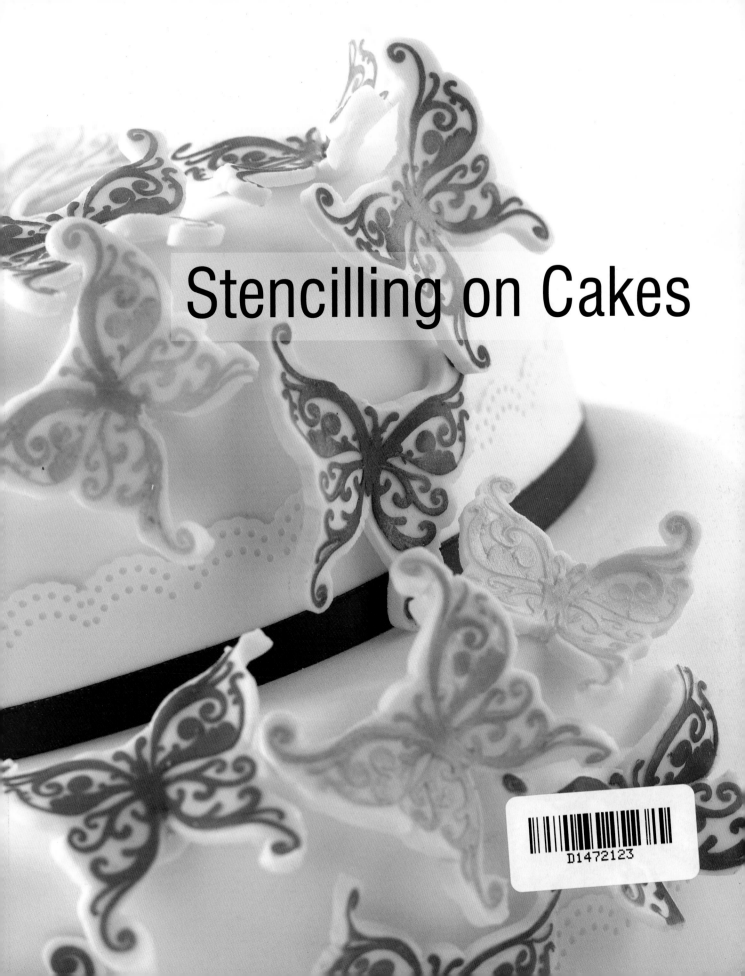

Stencilling on Cakes

Dedication

This book is dedicated to
everyone who has a dream.
Follow your dreams and
never give up. Dreams do
come true.

Stencilling on Cakes

Stephanie Weightman

SEARCH PRESS

First published in Great Britain 2013

Search Press Limited
Wellwood, North Farm Road,
Tunbridge Wells, Kent TN2 3DR

ISBN: 978-1-84448-952-7

Suppliers

If you have difficulty in obtaining any of the materials and equipment mentioned in this book, then please visit the Search Press website for details of suppliers:
www.searchpress.com

You are also invited to visit the author's websites:
www.stephanieweightman.co.uk
www.mycupcakeclub.co.uk

Publisher's note

All the step-by-step photographs in this book feature the author, Stephanie Weightman, demonstrating how to add stencilled decoration to cakes. No models have been used.

Printed in China

CONTENTS

INTRODUCTION

Baking in my family goes back generations and I grew up with the smell of baking in the house. My mum's fairy cakes were the stuff of legend and my nan's coffee and walnut cake was truly memorable. As soon as I was tall enough to help I was allowed to stir in ingredients and would spend hours watching the oven to see when the cakes had risen so we could plan what decoration they would have. Cakes were not just for special occasions – there was always a full tin in the pantry. In fact, I still have my nan's old cake tin and often store cakes in it myself. I remember looking into it as a child, standing with my brother and trying to choose the prettiest of the cakes within.

Baking for me is all in the anticipation – and of course the pleasure in eating the finished cake and seeing others enjoy my creations. My home is very much the same: for me, decorating has always been my motivation. Whether interior design or baking, I can spend hours wrapped up in my own world of colours, styles and textures. I love to see a plate of pretty cupcakes on the kitchen table decorated to share with eager recipients, and larger cakes are a blank canvas, their tops and sides ready to be embellished. Differently and quirkily shaped cakes are also a wonderful way to display your decoration.

I am lucky to have spent my whole working life in creative environments. Spending years working and experimenting with paint led me to develop my own range of stencils and it was not long before I was hooked. The idea of being able to blend and add colour while creating a pattern or picture was like magic to me and I still get excited by the anticipation of removing the stencil to reveal a beautiful result.

You may be familiar with stencilling as something we do on walls and furniture, but as the process only involves having a good bleedproof contact with the surface to be decorated and the application of colour or texture through the design, why should we not stencil on food?

Stencilling is one of the fastest ways of decorating a cake to create a wow factor. Each design can be a mini work of art. By using different colours, different edible mediums and different stencil designs you can create colourful, classic or three-dimensional cakes. Experiment on different surfaces – edible ones, of course! You do not have to be an expert to achieve exceptional professional results.

Stencils come in all shapes and sizes. Do not be limited by thinking the stencil has to be the exact size of the cake you are decorating. Sometimes I only use a small part of a large design, you will be surprised how many different looks you can get by doing this. With stencilling you do not have to be an artist, or in fact an experienced cake decorator this is something that you could be doing for the very first time.

MATERIALS

There is a wide range of materials available for cake decorating. However, all the cakes in this book can be made and decorated with a small, traditional range of cake tins and the readily available tools described on the following pages.

Cake

Fruit cakes – the most traditional type of cake to decorate – are normally quite heavy and dense, with a relatively low flour but high fruit content. They store well.

A basic Victoria sandwich recipe is buttery, spongy and light. It is perfect for large, small or cupcake-sized cakes and can be cut and shaped when cool. This delicate cake can be flavoured with vanilla extract or orange or lemon zest.

Chocolate cake can be light and fluffy or dense and moist. Either way, it does not often last long enough to worry about storage, but it will normally keep well for four to five days.

Cake tins come in all shapes and sizes. Some are coated with a non-stick surface while others require you to line the tin or use paper cases. Check your recipe for the most suitable method. If you are only going to use a special shaped tin once, you might consider hiring it from your local cake decorating shop.

Clockwise from top left: a square Victoria sandwich, a fruit cake, cupcakes and chocolate cake.

Cake coverings

Sugarpaste, also called sugarpaste icing or fondant icing, is very sweet, edible sugar dough which is usually made from sugar and glucose and available coloured or white. You can add food colouring to white icing to tint it to the colour you want.

Royal icing is a hard, white icing made from softly beaten egg whites, icing sugar and sometimes lemon or lime juice. It is applied to the cake (normally marzipan-covered in advance) while liquid.

Buttercream is a type of icing used inside cakes both as a coating and as decoration. It is made using butter, icing sugar, vanilla and sometimes milk.

Marzipan is a paste of ground almonds, sugar and egg whites, mostly used to cover cakes before icing. It can be used for modelling and you can paint and stencil directly on to it. Fruit preserve can be used to help secure the marzipan to the cake.

Icing sugar is a very fine powdered sugar used to make icing, or sprinkled to prevent other items from sticking to work surfaces

Sugar sheets are very finely rolled icing that is pliable and easy to handle. They should be kept in an airtight bag between uses to prevent them from drying out. The paper backing needs to be removed before use.

Cocoa is very fine and powdery and can be used for dusting and mixed into buttercream to give a rich chocolatey taste.

Chocolate is a great medium in cake decorating. Not only can it be melted to cover a cake, it can also be drizzled to create patterns or melted and mixed into the cake mixture.

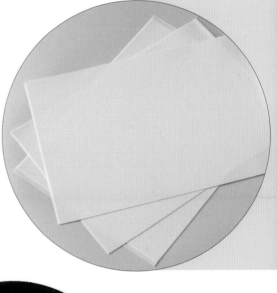

Clockwise from top left: coloured buttercream, pure buttercream, sugarpaste in various colours, royal icing in a piping bag (with an alternative nozzle), cocoa powder, chocolate and fruit preserve. The inset shows sugarpaste sheets.

Painting and colouring materials

The colours we add to our cakes should be edible powders, liquids and gels unless used on a removable decoration. Edible dusting powder food colours can be used on their own or mixed with edible confectioner's glaze or varnish to create edible paint. You can create an almost infinite number of shades by combining different powder food colours.

Nylon bristle brushes are the most hygienic for painting on to cakes. You will need an assortment of sizes, and you should clean the brushes between each application to stop the colours from becoming muddy.

To clean your brushes and remove edible varnish, food grade alcohol or isopropyl can be used.

Stencilling materials

When using stencils, sometimes known as templates, to decorate your cakes, hygiene must be considered, so stencils should be made from food grade plastic or material and cleaned after every application. The ready-made stencils used in this book are available through all good stockists.

If you are cutting your own stencils (see page 30) they need to be made from acetate which is readily available from most craft shops. You will also need a glass (or otherwise heatproof) mat and a stencil cutter which can be bought from a general craft shop. Always plan your stencil design before attempting to cut out, find an image you would like to use and print it out so you can trace it using the stencil cutter, you need to make sure there are enough bridges in the stencil to stop the design falling apart.

You will need a roller to create a perfectly smooth surface on your cake prior to decorating and to emboss the stencils into the surface. Rolling pins come in lots of different sizes. Plastic ones are easy to keep clean and being straight, do not leave marks on the icing. White vegetable fat is used to prevent icing from sticking to your work surface when you roll it out: smooth a small amount on to the work surface before you start.

Spacers are lengths of plastic laid on the surface next to your icing. You then roll the roller over them to ensure an even thickness to your icing.

Other materials

In addition to the main materials listed on the previous pages, you will need a few other items.

Palettes are good for keeping your colours separate.

Craft punches are a good alternative to decorating with ribbon when used in conjunction with sugar sheets.

Greaseproof paper protects surfaces and is used to line cake tins.

Rulers are used both for measuring and making straight line impressions.

Palette knives in various sizes are used to lift rolled icing on to cupcakes and cakes and also to smooth royal icing or buttercream.

A pastry brush is used to brush fruit preserves on to cakes.

Various sizes of scissors are useful to cut sugarpaste sheets and baking parchment. Scissors with a non-stick coating are ideal.

Circle cutters are perfect for cutting toppers on cupcakes and for plaques. They can also be used to cut sugarpaste sheets to shape.

Edible glue is used to stick two icing surfaces together

Kitchen paper is used to dry brushes and clean up.

A turntable is useful, although not essential, when cake decorating. Choose one with a tilting feature.

Keep a variety of cupcake cases and decorative cupcake wraps in your store cupboard, as they can be the finishing touch when it comes to coordinating the cake design with table decorations.

Cake boards are used to present celebration cakes. The board is normally covered with icing and edged with ribbon to complement your design.

A worktop or food board with non-slip backing is essential.

Masking tape is used to secure stencils in place.

A sharp kitchen knife can be used to cut through icing without leaving rough edges.

Various widths, colours and designs of ribbon are used for decorating cake bases and boards.

Smeared in a thin layer, white vegetable fat helps prevent icing sticking to your surface and stencils.

Shaping tools are perfect for moulding and shaping sugarpaste.

If you have a selection of coloured icing, a variety of small bowls to keep the colours separate is useful.

Sticky tape or low-tack sticky tape is used to attach ribbons to the surface of cake boards for a perfect finish.

A smoother is a flat-faced tool you can use over the surface of your cake to create a perfect finish.

A craft knife is always useful in cake decoration for fine details.

String is used to help measure around large cakes when stencilling the sides.

Use glass-headed pins to temporarily secure ribbons and stencils in place on cakes. You can cover any holes they leave with a small amount of icing and a little water.

A powder dredger is used to sprinkle icing sugar on to surfaces prior to rolling out, and also to dust cocoa on to the stencils.

A shaping mat is a bumpy foam mat used to help develop the shapes of flowers, butterflies and other small sugarpaste pieces.

TECHNIQUES

Stencils can be used in many ways and with different surfaces. Whether your preferred choice is sugarpaste, royal icing, buttercream or chocolate, all cake coverings can be adapted to achieve stunning effects.

Cake covering

A perfectly covered cake is an ideal surface to stencil upon. Covering your chosen cake with sugarpaste will help to give you a professional-looking smooth base for the other techniques.

Sugarpaste

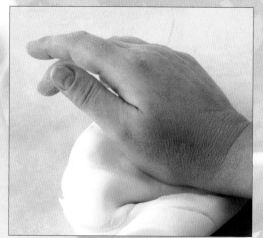

1 Knead the sugarpaste using the heel of your hand until it becomes smooth and workable.

2 Cover the surface with white vegetable fat, then put down your spacers (see inset) and roll out the sugarpaste. The spacers help to ensure you get a uniform thickness to the icing.

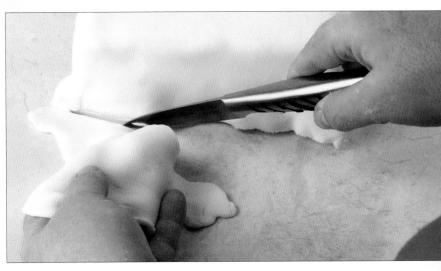

3 Cover the cake so that there is a small skirt of icing around every edge as shown.

4 Pull in the skirt and trim it away using a sharp knife.

5 Using a smoother, smooth the icing over the whole cake. Trim away any excess from the bottom, if necessary, using a sharp kitchen knife.

The covered cake in place on a cake board.

Cutting a sugarpaste plaque

This technique shows you how to add an extra dimension with a simple layering effect using sugarpaste. Plaques are also useful because you can decorate them quite intricately and then place the finished piece on top of an iced cake.

1 Knead the sugarpaste, cover your surface with white vegetable fat and roll it out, as on page 12. Once the sugarpaste is ready, carefully place your template over the top. Here I am using a small plate for the template.

2 Trim away any excess icing with a sharp knife, using the plate as a template.

3 Lift away the plate and carefully slide the palette knife under the icing plaque.

4 Supporting the plaque with your hand and palette knife, lift it up and place it on your cake. Carefully slide the knife out from underneath.

The finished plaque, placed on a cake covered with sugarpaste.

Royal icing

When working with royal icing, it is important that your cake has a smooth surface. Marzipan is ideal on a fruit cake to level off and hide the bumps before you apply the icing.

1 Warm your jam a little in the microwave or in a saucepan, then use a pastry brush to apply a generous coat over your cake.

Tip
If your fruit cake has lost a currant or has a small hole you can fill it with a small piece of marzipan and coat the jam over the top.

2 Use a palette knife to move your cake to one side, then dust the surface with icing sugar and cover your cake with marzipan, following the technique for sugarpaste on page 12.

3 Pick the cake up and put it on a cake board, then put the cake board on top of a turntable. Prepare your royal icing and pick up a measure on your palette knife, then put it on top of the cake.

4 Allow the icing to flow down the sides, adding more icing to the top if necessary, then smooth it down using a clean palette knife.

5 Once the royal icing has developed a slight crust (generally after ten or fifteen minutes), dampen your palette knife and smooth the icing once more. Hold the knife upright in the correct position and rotate the turntable to help you.

The finished cake, covered with royal icing and placed on a cake board.

Sugarpaste sheets

Using sugarpaste sheets adds a certain depth and dimension to your cake decorating. A very versatile way to decorate your cakes, this technique lends itself to almost any occasion or celebration.

1 Remove the plastic protective layer from the decorated sugar sheet and place it on a hard surface. Press the cutter down over the image.

2 Once you can feel that you have cut through the sheet, continue pressing down and rotate the cutter to cut cleanly.

3 Carefully lift out the small plaque and place it to one side. Make a second in the same way. This will become the shaped piece.

4 For the shaped piece, cut away any excess icing with your non-stick scissors, then trim around the shape, leaving a fine border.

 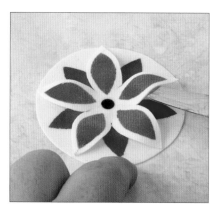 

5 Place both pieces on a shaping mat and tease the petals of the shaped piece gently into shape using the palette knife.

6 Allow the shaped piece to dry for a few minutes, then gently attach it to the small plaque, using a touch of water or edible glue.

The plaque placed on top of a cupcake covered with sugarpaste.

Using chocolate

Who can resist chocolate sugarpaste, chocolate cake or even melted chocolate? They are simply heaven! Pour melted chocolate over a cupcake and let it run down the sides for a more indulgent finish.

1 Gently warm good-quality chocolate either in your microwave or over a pan of boiling water, being careful to ensure the chocolate does not boil. Allow it to cool to a semi-glossy consistency that drizzles as shown.

2 Use a teaspoon to lift some chocolate on to your cupcake, and use the back of the spoon to smooth it into place.

A cupcake covered with chocolate.

Piped ganache

Create stunning results when you pipe with ganache. So simple yet effective, it is a more luxurious finish than using just buttercream and helps to create that wow factor every time!

1 Mix melted chocolate and double cream to make chocolate ganache, and fill a piping bag with it. Use a flower nozzle on the icing bag.

2 Bring the bag to the centre of the cupcake and gently squeeze out a central point.

3 Without releasing the pressure, slowly work anti-clockwise around the central point.

4 Continue working around until you have covered the whole top, then gradually release the pressure as you work and lift the nozzle away.

A cupcake covered with piped chocolate ganache.

Piped chocolate ganache and vanilla buttercream

A lovely marbled effect can be achieved by placing chocolate ganache and buttercream together in the same piping bag.

1 Take a piping bag with a flower nozzle and use a palette knife to fill half of it with vanilla buttercream.

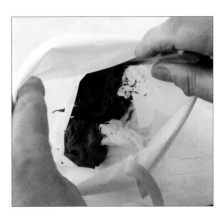

2 Fill the other half with chocolate ganache.

3 Bring the bag to the centre of the cupcake and gently squeeze out a central point.

4 Without releasing the pressure, slowly work anti-clockwise around the central point.

5 Continue working around until you have covered the whole top, then gradually release the pressure as you work and lift the nozzle away.

A cupcake covered with piped chocolate ganache and vanilla buttercream.

STENCILLING TECHNIQUES

There are a variety of ways to use stencils in cake decoration, from creating simple embossing to sumptuous blended colour effects. All sorts of icing, ganache, chocolate and even buttercream can be used with stencils to great effect, and with the right equipment you can cut your own stencils to create unique and individual designs.

The following pages cover the versatile basic techniques used throughout the book.

Embossing

1 Lay a thin layer of white vegetable fat over the work surface, then knead a small amount of sugarpaste and roll it out to a thickness of no less than 5mm (¼in) using a small rolling pin.

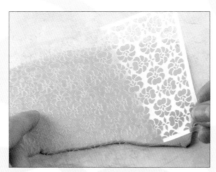

2 Carefully lay the embossing stencil flat on top of the icing.

3 Roll the small rolling pin firmly over the stencil and sugarpaste.

4 Peel away the stencil carefully.

A cupcake covered with embossed sugarpaste.

Dusting

1 Follow steps one and two for embossing (see opposite), and leave the stencil in place.

2 Lightly brush a contrasting colour of edible dusting powder over the whole piece using a soft flat brush. Aim to cover a piece slightly larger than the size of your cutter.

3 Continue brushing the powder into the surface until it has all been worked in; this ensures the piece will remain clean when you lift away the stencil.

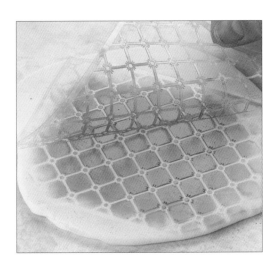

4 Carefully peel away the stencil.

A cupcake covered with embosssed and dusted sugarpaste.

Blending colours

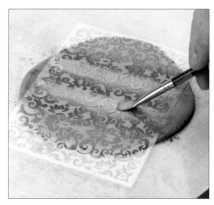

1 Follow steps one and two for embossing (see page 20), and leave the stencil in place. Brush on your first colour of edible dusting powder in bold stripes.

2 Change to a clean brush and brush on a complementary colour of edible dusting powder between the stripes.

3 Still using the brush with the second colour, blend the boundaries of the stripes together until all the powder has been worked in.

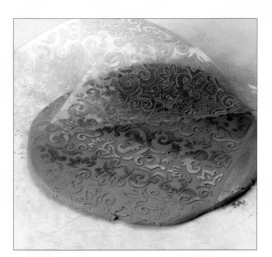

4 Peel the stencil away carefully.

A cupcake covered with embossed sugarpaste coloured with blended gold and purple.

Picking out elements of a design

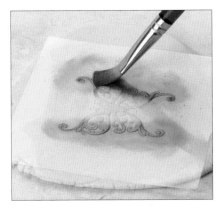

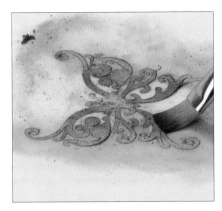

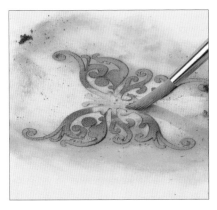

1 Follow steps one and two for embossing (see page 20), and leave the stencil in place. Using a small flat brush and your first colour of edible dusting powder, pick out some of the details of the design, working from the outside of the stencil inwards. In this instance, I am using metallic pink.

2 Using a clean brush and a second colour (mulberry here), work closer towards the centre of the design, blending the powder into the previous colour.

3 Blend in a third colour (metallic purple here) to the central part of the design. Use a size 5 clean round brush to pick out any small details.

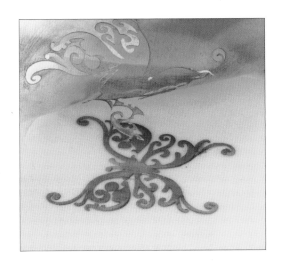

4 Gently brush any excess powder away from the design, being careful not to blur the image, then peel away the stencil.

A cupcake decorated with sugarpaste and a decorative butterfly.

Cutting out a stencilled design

1 Follow steps 1–4 for blending (see page 22) using electric blue and metallic light silver edible dusting powders.

2 Hold a sharp craft knife with a clean disposable blade perpendicular to the surface. Begin to trim carefully around the design, working up to the edges.

3 Cut away large sections of excess sugarpaste to make it easier to cut closely to the design.

4 Use a palette knife to carefully lift the whole design away from the surface, ready to use.

A square cake covered with sugarpaste, with a sugarpaste design in place.

Stencilling on buttercream

1 Mix your buttercream and apply a layer to the top of the cupcake. Smooth it using a warm palette knife, then place it in the refrigerator until it hardens and forms a crust.

2 Gently place the stencil on top of the cupcake.

3 Using a powder dredger filled with cocoa powder, dust the cake thoroughly.

4 Cover the whole cake (see inset) then carefully lift away the stencil.

A cupcake covered with chocolate-decorated buttercream.

Placing a design on the side of a cake

1 Place the stencil on the side of the cake and use pins to hold it in place temporarily.

2 Mix melted chocolate and double cream to make chocolate ganache, and use a palette knife to apply a fairly large amount to the centre of the stencil.

3 Remove the pins and use the palette knife to spread the ganache thinly over the whole area.

4 Carefully peel away the stencil to reveal the pattern.

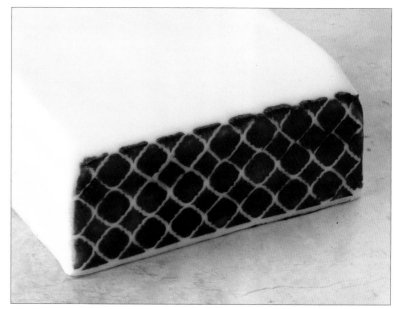

A square cake covered with sugarpaste, with a stencilled design in chocolate ganache on one side.

Wet colour

1 Follow steps one and two for embossing (see page 20), and leave the stencil in place. Pick up green colouring gel on a medium (size 2) stencilling brush and stipple it on to a piece of kitchen paper to remove the excess gel.

2 Very softly stipple over the whole stencil except for the flower petals, as shown.

3 Load a clean size 2 stencilling brush with red colouring gel. Stipple it on to a piece of kitchen paper as before to remove excess gel, then very lightly stipple the flower petals.

4 Carefully lift away the stencil.

A cupcake covered with sugarpaste, decorated with wet colouring gel.

Shaping individual elements

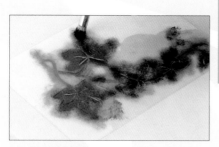

1 Remove the plastic protective layer from the decorated sugar sheet, then put a thin layer of white vegetable fat over your stencil and place it on top. Colour your stencil – here I am using leaf green food gel and a size 2 stencilling brush. Add some variation to the colour by using golden yellow in the centres of the leaves and royal blue food gel at the very tips.

2 Carefully remove the stencil, then cut around one of the tips of the large central leaf (see inset), and gently lift it away from the surface using the flat of the blade.

3 Remove the knife blade and slide a cone-shaped sculpting tool in its place. Use the craft knife to gently ease the tip of the leaf around the cone-shaped tool.

Tip
Do not clean your brush betwen colours, as this helps to ensure that the colours complement each other.

4 Repeat the process over the parts of the design that you want to stand out.

The finished plaque placed as a centrepiece on an iced round cake.

Stencil decoupage

1 With a decorated plaque in place, make a copy of the stencil you used by following step one for shaping individual elements (see opposite). Carefully cut out the elements to be decoupaged using a pair of non-stick scissors.

2 Cut out all of the elements ready to be used, then place them on a shaping mat. Use your fingers to gently curve the tips of the leaves (or appropriate details of other designs).

3 Prepare a tiny ball of sugarpaste and place it on the decorated plaque (see inset), then place one of the prepared elements on top, pressing down slightly to secure the element to the sugarpaste.

4 Place the other elements in the same way.

The centrepiece plaque opposite has been developed with additional leaves to build up a three-dimensional structure.

Cutting your own stencils

1 With a glass mat to protect your work surface, place a sheet of acetate over your template.

2 Use low-tack tape to secure the acetate to the template while your hot stencil cutting tool is warming up. Next, use the tool like a pen to draw round the template.

3 Continue drawing round every detail of the template until you have finished. Remove the tape and then carefully lift the cut-out template away.

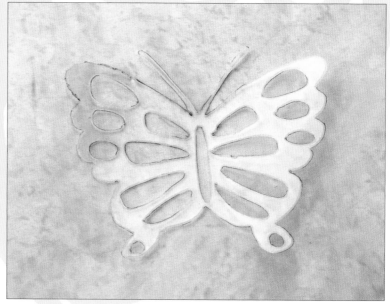

4 You may need to remove internal parts of the template. If so, simply pull them gently until they come away. As long as you have cut round them, they should come out easily.

A completed stencil.

Stencilling on chocolate

1 Take a chocolate-covered cupcake that has cooled and set completely. Place your stencil on top.

2 Pick up some buttercream on your palette knife and place it in the centre. Gently draw the buttercream outwards to the edge and off in one smooth movement.

3 Rotate the cupcake, pick up more buttercream and repeat the process.

4 Carefully remove the stencil.

A cupcake covered with chocolate, with a buttercream design in place.

Pattern matching

1 Using scissors, carefully trim away any border on your stencil.

2 Knead white sugarpaste using the heel of your hand until it becomes smooth and workable, then cover the surface with white vegetable fat, put down your spacers and roll out the sugarpaste. Place your stencil on top and roll firmly over it with a large rolling pin.

3 Carefully remove the stencil, then replace it, matching the existing embossed detail to the detail on the stencil to help you position it perfectly in place.

4 Use a small rolling pin with a chamfered edge to roll firmly over the stencil, being careful not to roll over the previously embossed detail.

5 Carefully remove the stencil and repeat the process to the end of the icing.

6 Using a spacer as a straight edge, cut away the excess icing with a sharp kitchen knife.

The completed sheet of embossed sugarpaste.

PATTERNED CUPCAKES

This simple technique – of interchanging different coloured icing in a pattern on a small cupcake – creates a stunning and unusual effect. Experiment with your colours to get a different look every time.

You will need

Vintage flock stencil

1 or more cupcakes

Edible dusting powder in metallic blue

Green and blue sugarpaste

Smoother

Rolling pin and spacers

15mm (⅝in) flat brush

Circle cutter and kitchen knife

White vegetable fat

1 Cover the surface with white vegetable fat and roll out green sugarpaste, using spacers to ensure the depth is uniform. Trim away the side with a sharp kitchen knife to leave a straight edge.

2 Roll out and trim your blue sugarpaste in the same way and abut the pieces. Use a smoother to gently bond them together into a uniform surface.

3 Place the stencil on top of the sugarpaste surface and firmly roll over it.

4 Use a 15mm (⅝in) flat brush with metallic blue edible dusting powder to colour an area of the stencil large enough to cut out, then remove the stencil.

5 Use the circle cutter to cut out a circle, then place it on top of the cupcake.

Detail from the Patterned Cupcakes, shown opposite. This technique is easily adapted to give a striped effect, by trimming one colour into a thin strip and abutting pieces on either side, or to give a patchwork effect by smoothing small squares together.

Opposite

The finished cupcake alongside others made with the same techniques. Vintage flock, filigree swirl, vibrant vines, rose and swirly stencils were used with various colours and combinations of sugarpaste pieces.

LACY CUPCAKES

These cupcakes are created using a simple blending technique. When blending, always ensure you use the lightest colour first. Clean your brush between each application to keep the colours sharp and stop them muddying.

You will need

Butterfly Lace stencil
1 or more cupcakes
White sugarpaste
Edible dusting powder
in metallic red and gold
5mm (¼in) flat brush
7.5cm (3in) circle cutter
Spacers and rolling pin
White vegetable fat

 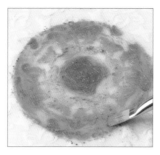  

1 Cover the surface with white vegetable fat and roll out white sugarpaste, using spacers to ensure the depth is uniform. Use the roller to emboss the surface with the stencil, ensuring the focal point of the design is central on your icing.

2 Use the 5mm (¼in) flat brush to colour the centre (or focal point) with dusting powder. Start in the centre with metallic red, then circle this with gold without cleaning your brush. Repeat for the outer part with metallic red.

3 Carefully remove the stencil and place the circle cutter on top, ensuring the focal point is in the exact centre.

4 Use the circle cutter to cut out the icing and place it on top of the cupcake.

Right
Detail from the Lacy Cupcakes, shown opposite. By altering where you put the colours, a variety of blended designer cupcakes can be made.

SINGLE TIER CAKE WITH DAISY FLOWERS

This cake has been decorated using a spot lustre technique which can be adapted to large and small cakes with ease. Contrasting colours work well together to create a dramatic effect.

You will need

Floral Burst stencil

30cm (12in) round cake covered with white sugarpaste

10mm (⅜in), 12mm (½in), and 15mm (⅝in) flat brushes

Edible dusting powder in white, yellow, light green, dark green, purple and pearl white

Kitchen paper

Large rolling pin

White vegetable fat

1 Place your stencil on top of the iced cake and emboss the design into the surface using a rolling pin.

2 Begin to establish the base image by colouring the tips of the leaves near the narrow-petalled flower with light green edible dusting powder and the 12mm (½in) flat brush.

3 Without cleaning the brush, build up the stems and bases of some of the leaves to create some shading using the dark green powder.

4 Change to a clean 15mm (⅝in) brush and use purple powder to colour the flowers. Put the brush to one side.

5 Change to a 10mm (⅜in) flat brush. Pick up yellow on the brush and colour the petals of the third foreground flower, working from the outside in. Pick up a little white on the brush when you reload to soften the colour a little.

The finished Single Tier Cake with Daisy Flowers, along with two cupcakes decorated using the same techniques and a smaller complementary stencil.

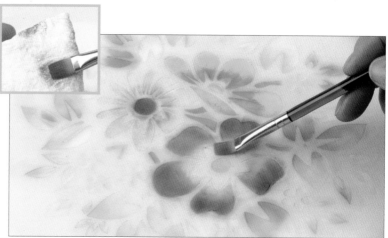

6 Pick up an even mix of white and yellow on the same brush and colour the smaller background flowers. Without cleaning the brush, pick up white and colour the remaining parts of the foreground flowers.

7 Pick up the brush with a little purple remaining on it (from step 4), and gently blend the colours together on the foreground flowers. The tiny amount of colour remaining on the brush will softly tint the petals. As the colour runs out, you will need to reload the brush with purple. Wipe away most of the powder on kitchen paper to ensure you retain a subtle effect (see inset).

8 Still using the same brush, use a sweeping motion to begin to blend the leaves together. Sweep the brush across the tips of a whole group of leaves to bind them together and give a cohesive feel. Differentiating the leaves across the design helps add depth to the design.

9 Pick up a little purple and light green on the brush and mix them together on a spare lid or the work surface. Use a little of this mix to soften any particularly strong colours remaining on the design, such as the very bright yellow background flowers.

10 With the blending completed, very gently overlay the whole image with pearl white and a light circular motion to soften the colour a little more, then carefully remove the stencil to finish (see inset).

Opposite

Details from the Daisy Flower cake and cupcakes decorated in a similar way.

TRELLIS CAKE

This project shows how stylish using buttercream can be through a larger stencil. The same stencil has been used on the ribbon embellishment to create a sophisticated look.

You will need

30cm (12in) and 20cm (8in)
Large Decorative Trellis stencils
30cm (12in) and 20cm (8in) square cakes,
both covered with lilac sugarpaste
15mm (⅝in) flat brush
Edible dusting powder in metallic purple
Palette knife and kitchen knife
Ivory sugarpaste, rolling pin and spacers
Buttercream
30mm (1⅛in) circle cutters
White vegetable fat and edible glue

1 Put the smaller cake on top of the larger. Pin the 30cm (12in) stencil to the side of the larger cake and use the palette knife to apply buttercream to each side in turn. Repeat the process on the smaller cake with the 20cm (8in) stencil.

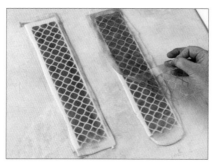

2 Cover the surface with white fat and roll out ivory sugarpaste into a long strip. Use the rolling pin to emboss the surface with the 30cm (12in) stencil. Use the very large flat brush to apply metallic purple edible dusting powder. Remove the stencil and make a second piece in the same way.

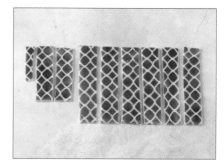

3 Use a sharp kitchen knife to trim away any excess sugarpaste so you have two wide pieces completely covered by the pattern. Next, cut the pieces into the following smaller strips: six 13 x 2.5cm (5⅛ x 1in); two 9 x 2.5cm (3½ x 1in); and one 5 x 1.5cm (2 x ½in).

4 Carefully wrap one of the 13cm (5⅛in) strips around the 30mm (1⅛in) circle cutter. Apply a little edible glue to glue the ends together, then use a sharp knife to cut away any excess icing and to trim away the corners of the fused piece.

5 Repeat the process for the remaining five 13cm (5⅛in) strips and leave them to dry for an hour. While you wait, curl the smallest strip into a horseshoe shape and trim the ends, then drape the two longer strips over 30mm (1⅛in) circle cutters and cut the ends as shown.

6 Arrange five of the prepared loops in the centre of the top of the cake and then slip one of the longer strips into the space. Place the second long strip over the first, and use a sharp knife to trim away where they overlap.

7 Set the final loop in place over the two longer strips, then add the tiny loop in the centre.

FOOTBALL CAKE

Something for the boys! This project shows how a simple design can be used on large cakes and cupcakes alike with striking effects. The black colour gives the cakes a stunning effect. Make this, and you will score a perfect finish every time.

You will need

Large Football stencil

30cm (12in) round cake covered with white sugarpaste

Very large 15mm (⅝in) flat brush

Edible dusting powder in black and silver

White sugarpaste

Icing sugar and powder dredger

Large rolling pin and kitchen knife

Baking parchment

White vegetable fat

1 Lay out baking parchment on your surface, and use a powder dredger to scatter icing sugar over the surface. Knead your white sugarpaste and roll it out into a circle as close in size to the stencil as possible, not less than 5mm (¼in) thick, then lay the stencil on top. Use the large rolling pin to roll over the whole design.

2 Colour the icing using the 15mm (⅝in) flat brush and black dusting powder, working from the centre outwards. Without cleaning the brush, lightly brush silver powder over the lighter side to develop the highlights and give the ball a sense of roundness.

3 Use a sharp knife to cut around the edge of the stencil, then very carefully remove the offcuts, icing sugar and loose edible dusting powder, brushing them into the dustbin. It is important that your work area and stencil is as clean as possible before removing the stencil.

4 Remove the stencil, then pick up the sheet of baking parchment, supporting the football beneath with your hand. Place it on top of the cake and slowly roll the baking parchment under itself, allowing the football to slide on to the top of the cake.

5 Continue rolling the parchment up, ensuring that the football is sitting correctly on top of the cake to finish.

The Football Cake along with cupcakes decorated in a similar way.

CAMEO CAKE

Cameos are always a favourite and look stunning layered on to different colours of icing in this timeless wedding cake project. This project also shows you how to stencil directly on to the cake using a large stencil, and how to fill in areas that the stencil can not reach in one go.

1 Wrap the *Filigree Swirl* stencil all the way round the 30cm (12in) cake and pin it in place. If your stencil does not reach, then take a piece of string and cut a length equal to the gap between the pattern – note that this is not the ends of the stencil. Put the piece of string to one side.

2 Cover the stencil with buttercream following the instructions on page 25, but substituting the chocolate with blue buttercream. Carefully remove the stencil, wash it clean and let it dry.

3 Use your scissors to cut a length of the stencil equal to the length of the string from step 1. Ensure you do not keep any of the outside border. Pin this piece in the gap, following the instructions for pattern matching on page 32.

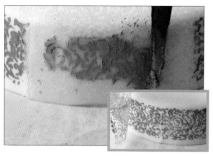

4 Secure the stencil in place with blue buttercream in the centre, remove the pins and cover the rest of the border. Once dry, carefully remove the stencil (see inset).

5 Roll out a small amount of white sugarpaste to a thickness of 3mm (⅛in). Place the cameo stencil on top. Use a 15mm (⅝in) flat brush to dust the whole stencil area with light blue dusting powder, then pick up a little silver on the same brush and lightly dust the portrait.

The finished Cameo Cake would be perfect for a wedding.

6 Use the oval side of the double-sided cutter to cut round the portrait.

7 Prepare and roll out some baby blue sugarpaste, then use the scalloped side of the double-sided cutter to cut out a scalloped oval. Pick up the portrait oval on your palette knife and place it carefully on top of the scalloped oval. Make five more of these and leave them to dry.

8 Cut out an oval from white sugarpaste using the large double-sided cutter, and put one of the five assembled pieces on top. Turn over the cutter and cut out a large scalloped oval from baby blue sugarpaste and place the assembled piece on top to complete the cameo. Make five more of these for a total of eleven cameos (five with one layer of backing and six larger ones with three layers of backing)

9 Place the 25.5cm (10in) and 20cm (8in) cakes on top of the larger cake. Wrap the bottom of each new layer with light blue organza ribbon, then wrap slightly mid-blue ribbon over the top of the light blue ribbons.

10 Secure one of the larger cameos to the middle tier of the cake using edible glue.

11 Take an icing bag with a size 2 round nozzle and fill it with royal icing. Use a tiny dab of icing to attach an edible pearl into each scallop of the background layer.

12 Secure the larger plaques evenly around the middle tier and the smaller plaques evenly around the upper tier.

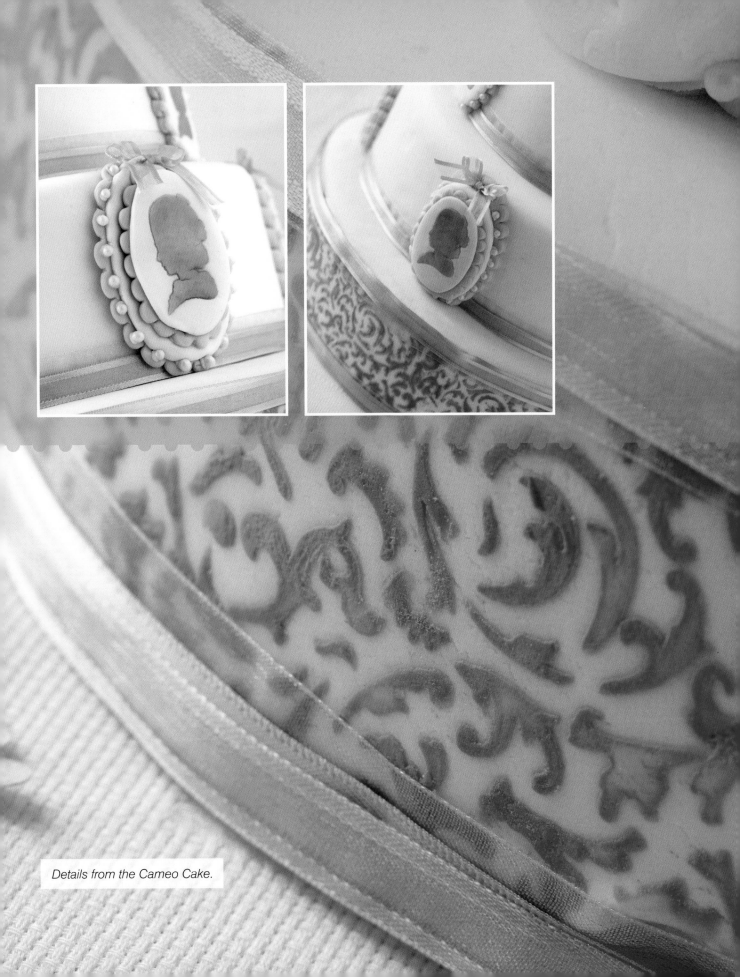

Details from the Cameo Cake.

BUTTERFLY CASCADE

Stencilled on to a thin layer of sugarpaste and then cut out before being added to the cake with edible glue, this cascade of butterflies is perfect for a little princess, whether it is her birthday or her wedding.

You will need

Decorative Butterfly stencil

30cm (12in) and 20cm (8in) round cakes, both covered with white sugarpaste

Edible dusting powder in maroon, metallic purple and light bue

Craft powder in electric blue

Sticky tape

Border craft punch

Non-stick scissors

Edible glue

Purple ribbon

White sugarpaste

Sticky tape

Shaping mat

White sugarpaste sheets

Icing tube with size 3 nozzle

White royal icing

Kitchen knife

White vegetable fat

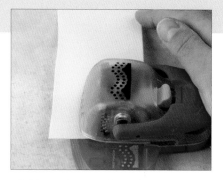

1 Place the smaller cake on top of the larger, setting it slightly off-centre. Cut a strip of sugar sheet slightly wider than your border craft punch, and remove the backing sheet. Slide the strip into your craft punch and press the lever down to punch the sheet.

2 Release the lever then, using the guide on the punch, slide the strip down and punch a border pattern along the strip.

3 Punch all the way to the end of the strip, then use non-stick scissors to trim the strip so that there is 2cm (¾in) of sugar sheet below the bottom of the pattern.

4 Make sufficient strips to go all the way around the base of both layers of the cake and attach them using edible glue.

5 Wrap a purple ribbon around the base of the top tier, attaching it with a little sticky tape.

The finished Butterfly Cascade and a cupcake made with the same colours and techniques.

6 Roll out a little white sugarpaste and follow the instructions on page 24 to make and cut out a large butterfly. Apply maroon dusting powder and electric blue craft powder to the butterfly, then blend the colours in and overlay them with light blue colouring powder. Remove the stencil.

7 Cut out the butterfly and place it on the shaping mat (see inset), then make a second large butterfly in the same way. Make three medium and at least eleven small butterflies, decorating them with the same colours as the larger ones. Vary the way you apply the colours for interest.

Tip
Craft powder is not edible, so only use it on removable elements.

Tip
Do not worry if one of the butterflies breaks – they will be overlaying each other, so minor breakages will be easy to hide.

8 Take an icing tube with a size 3 round nozzle and fill it with royal icing. Take one of the smaller butterflies and add a dab of royal icing to the centre of the back, then carefully apply the butterfly to the top of the cake.

9 Attach another butterfly on the side below the first. Use a pin to hold it in place while the icing dries, hiding it under the body of the butterfly.

10 Position some of the remaining butterflies on the cake in an attractive arrangement. Do not feel you need attach them all – any remaining can be in reserve in case of breakage, or they can be used on accompanying cupcakes.

Opposite
Details from the Butterfly Cascade and cupcake.

TREE OF LIFE

These instructions will result in a perfect retirement cake, showing how basic stencilling can be made to look dramatic and highly effective on a plain white cake.

You will need

Tree of Life, *Cottage Fence* and *Floral* stencils

30cm (12in) square cake, covered with white sugarpaste

Colouring gel in green, red and yellow

White sugarpaste sheets

Size 1 and 2 stencilling brushes

10mm (⅜in) flat brush

Edible glue

White vegetable fat and kitchen paper

1 Place the large tree stencil on top of the cake. Before doing anything else, check that the fence will fit well at the base of the tree later by holding the large fence stencil in place temporarily.

2 Once you are happy with the positioning, rub a light layer of white vegetable fat on the back of the large tree stencil and secure it in place on the top. Pick up some green colouring gel on a size 2 stencilling brush and stipple on to a spare piece of the stencil to remove some of the excess colour. Work towards the branches and stipple over the leaves, reloading the brush and removing the excess on kitchen paper as you work.

3 Without cleaning the brush, pick up a little red colouring gel. Dab it on to a spare part of the stencil, then pick up some green and mix the colour, using the spare part of the template as a palette. Add yellow if the brown mix is too dark.

4 Stipple the brown mix over the trunk and lower branches. Work up into the leaves a little to blend the colour areas, but be careful not to go too far with the brown as it is very strong.

5 Carefully remove the stencil. Leave the colour to dry, then put the fence stencil in place over the tree. Using the same brown mix and brush as before, stipple over the fence stencil.

6 Remove the stencil and leave to dry before placing the small flower stencil on the lower left-hand side in front of the fence. Use a clean size 1 stencilling brush to stipple red colouring gel on the flowerheads, then change to another clean size 1 stencilling brush to stipple green colour gel on the stems and leaves.

The finished Tree of Life cake.

7 Carefully remove the stencil and place two more small flowers in front of the fence. Allow to dry then use the large flower stencil to partially overlay the right-most flowers to suggest depth.

8 Using the small tree stencil and the colours and techniques in steps 2–4, make eight small trees on sugarpaste sheets. Make four small fences in the same way, using the brown mix left over from the trees. Once dry, carefully cut out both the fences and trees as shown, leaving some of the sugarpaste sheet to support delicate areas.

9 With the techniques and colours from step 6, make twelve large flowers and four small flowers on sugarpaste sheets, and cut around them carefully. Again, leave a border around the delicate parts.

Tip

If you have some spare sugarpaste, make some spare trees, fences and flowers in case of breakage.

10 Peel the backing from two of the trees and use edible glue and a 10mm (⅜in) flat brush to stick them to one of the sides of the cake. Apply glue only to the area which will stick to the cake, and not to the tops of the branches.

11 Remove the backing from one of the fences and use edible glue to attach it to the centre of the side, over the trees. Next, remove the backing from one small and two large flowers and glue them in place over the fence.

12 Decorate the other sides using the same number of pieces on each. Arrange each side slightly differently for a pleasing effect.

Opposite
Details from the Tree of Life cake.

CHRISTMAS BAUBLE

The dramatic colours of these Christmas baubles stencilled on to sugarpaste are really offset by the bright white of the cake. This gives a stunning result and a flamboyant cake for the festive season.

You will need

Christmas Bauble stencils

20cm (8in) round cake, covered with white sugarpaste

White sugarpaste

Edible glitter in red and blue

Edible colouring powder in green and silver

10mm (⅜in) flat brush

Non-stick scissors

Size 6 round brush

White sugarpaste sheets

Kitchen knife

Edible glue

White vegetable fat

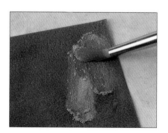

1 Knead and roll out a small amount of sugarpaste to a thickness of no less than 5mm (¼in) using a small rolling pin. Place one of the small bauble templates on top and roll it on to emboss the pattern. Use a 10mm (⅜in) flat brush to cover the stencil with edible glue.

2 Leave the glue for a few minutes until it becomes tacky, then pick up some red edible glitter on your finger and dab it in place, pressing it into the glue.

3 Once the bauble is covered, carefully remove the stencil and use a sharp knife to cut around the design.

4 Using the other two bauble stencils, make another two red baubles and three blue baubles using the same techniques. Place baubles on top of the cake. Where they overlap, use a kitchen knife to trim away the excess.

5 Use a size 6 round brush to apply green edible powder to a clean sugarpaste sheet. Once dry, overlay the sheet with silver edible powder.

6 Use a pair of non-stick scissors to cut six narrow strips and eight rectangles.

7 Make small triangular cuts into the sides of each rectangle to make x shapes.

8 Use edible glue to attach them to the cake. Run the strips into the baubles, trimming them with your scissors to fit, then apply the x shapes to the tops and bottoms of the strips.

The finished Christmas Bauble cake.

CHOCOLATE HEART

I love the contrast between the covered milk chocolate cake and the dark chocolate embossed stencilling. It is simple yet dramatic. The technique is very quick, and that makes this cake perfect when time is of the essence.

You will need

Budding Heart stencil

20cm (8in) heart-shaped cake covered with chocolate sugarpaste

Palette knife and dark chocolate

Large plate and white vegetable fat

1 Rub a thin layer of white vegetable fat over the back of the stencil and place it on top of the chocolate sugarpaste-covered cake. Warm some chocolate (see page 17), then temper the chocolate on a large plate. When the chocolate holds the lines you make with the palette knife, it is ready to apply.

2 Quickly pour a relatively small amount of chocolate on to the top of the stencil.

3 Working quickly, use your palette knife to spread the chocolate as thinly and smoothly as you can over the surface.

4 Before the chocolate sets, peel away the stencil to reveal the finished cake.

Tip

If the chocolate sets too quickly, warm the surface gently with a hairdryer.

The finished Chocolate Heart cake, along with a smaller cake made in the same way. Both have had matching gold and white ribbons added.

ELEGANT DOVE CAKE

Showcase your sugarcrafting techniques from stencilling to punch work to make this cake for occasions ranging from an engagement to a wedding, or from an anniversary to a big birthday.

You will need

Large and small *Dove* stencils

30cm (12in) oval cake, covered with white sugarpaste

Non-stick scissors

White sugarpaste sheets

Greaseproof paper

Gold edible lustre spray

Spacer

Edible dusting powder in gold and pink

20mm (¾in) and 15mm (⅝in) flat brushes

Gum tragacanth

Pink sugarpaste

Kitchen knife

Royal icing and icing bag with a size 2 round nozzle

Border craft punch

White vegetable fat

1 Use your non-stick scissors to trim one 9cm (3½in) strip and one 5cm (2in) wide strip of sugarpaste sheet. Use the craft punch to punch a decorative strip into each.

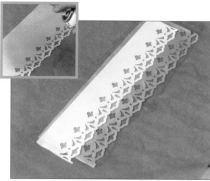

2 Lay down some greaseproof paper to protect your surface, then use gold edible lustre spray to coat the broader strip (see inset). While the spray is wet, lay the narrower strip on top.

3 Allow to dry, then use a spacer as a straight edge, carefully trim in a straight line just below the decorative edge of the narrow white strip. Make sufficient strips to go all the way around your cake.

4 Cut out a dove using the technique on page 24 and the large dove stencil, and decorate with gold and pink edible dusting powders. Apply the dusting powder with a 20mm (¾in) flat brush, and keep the pink more on the body, blending into gold on the wings.

Opposite
The finished Elegant Dove cake.

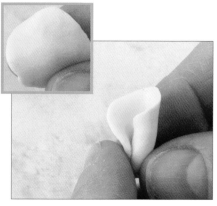

5 Turning the large dove stencil over, make a second large dove facing the other direction in the same way. Make three small doves with the small template with the same techniques, using a 15mm (⁵⁄₈in) flat brush, then attach the doves to the top of the cake with a touch of water. Wrap the strips around the outside of the cake using a tiny touch of water on the back to secure them.

6 Mix one teaspoon of gum tragacanth with 200g (7oz) pink sugarpaste, and pinch off seven pea-sized balls. Pinch the first ball into a small petal shape, making sure the leading edge is thin (see inset), then roll it up, with the leading edge slightly open as shown.

7 Pinch the second ball into a small petal as before, and roll it around the first, making sure to cover the join left in the first.

8 Continue building up the rose with the remaining balls, pinching each into fine petals and wrapping them around and covering the join of the previous one. As you reach the outer petals, peel the leading edges back a little as you wrap them (see inset). Continue until you have used all the balls.

9 Carefully trim away the base using a kitchen knife.

10 Make sufficient roses to surround the cake and attach them to the decorative strip with a dab of royal icing (applied using an icing bag with a size 2 round nozzle) on the bases.

Opposite

Details from the finished Elegant Dove cake.

FLORAL CAKE

This project combines two different techniques to great effect. The sugar sheets have been stencilled and built up using edible glue to create a decoupaged three-dimensional effect before being added to the already decorated cake.

You will need

Large Poinsettia, Small Poinsettia and *Filigree Swirl* stencils

30cm (12in) square cake, covered with white sugarpaste

Yellow buttercream

Large palette knife

Kitchen paper

Sugarpaste sheets

Colouring gels in red, yellow and green

Size 2 stippling brush

Icing bag with size 2 round nozzle

Royal icing

Red and yellow ribbons

Sticky tape

White vegetable fat

1 Rub a thin layer of white vegetable fat over the back of the *Filigree Swirl* stencil and place it on top of the covered cake. Use a large palette knife to spread the buttercream thinly over the top.

2 Remove the stencil and then wrap some kitchen paper around your finger. Gently draw your finger along the edge to remove any excess buttercream from the sides, then allow to dry.

The finished Floral Cake.

3 Using the large and small *Poinsettia* stencils, make at least ten small flowers and two large flowers from sugarpaste sheets, decorating them as described on page 27 using the size 2 stippling brush and red and yellow colouring gels. Use the same stencils to make ten large leaves and six small leaves from sugarpaste sheets; colouring them with green colouring gel and the size 2 stippling brush, then trimming the petals off as leaves.

67

4 Put a size 2 round nozzle into an icing bag and fill it with royal icing. Use this to attach one large flower and two small flowers in an arrangement on one of the corners of the cake.

Tip

If you have buttercream left over, you can fill the icing bag with buttercream and use that to attach the flowers and leaves.

5 Attach two small flowers and one large flower on top of the previous layer, rotating them slightly so that the petals fill the gaps in the previous layer. Tuck the large flower's petals underneath where they overlap the smaller flowers.

6 Layer the two small flowers with a further small flower on each, then put two layers of small flowers on top of the large flower.

7 Attach the leaves in the same way. Use a clean palette knife to gently lift the flowers as you tuck the leaves behind them.

8 Wrap a red ribbon round the sides of the cake, then a yellow ribbon around the red one. Attach both using a little sticky tape.

Opposite

Details from the finished Floral Cake.

CASCADING IVY

For this attractive and inviting cake, ivy leaves are stencilled on to sugarpaste before they are cut out and added to the cake. Along with some fine painted lines for the vines, this creates a beautiful effect. Look to nature for inspiration on how to lay the leaves on the cake for a more realistic result.

You will need

Ivy stencil

30cm (12in) and 20cm (8in) square cakes, covered with white sugarpaste

Edible dusting powders in light green, dark green, mid green, and autumn green

White sugarpaste sheets

Size 2 stencilling brush

Size 1 round brush

Non-stick scissors

Icing bag with size 2 round nozzle

White royal icing

White vegetable fat

Food grade alcohol

1 Put the smaller cake on top of the larger. Cut a sugar sheet down to the size of the template, and lay the ivy template on top. Use size 2 stencilling brushes to make small piles of light green and dark green edible dusting powder on a spare part of the stencil.

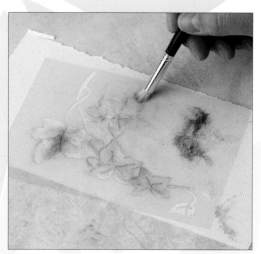

2 Use a size 2 stencilling brush to stipple light green into the centres of the ivy leaves, then tint the edges with a little dark green. Do not clean the brush in between to give a natural variegated effect.

3 Tap away any excess powder and carefully cut out the leaves using non-stick scissors.

Opposite

The finished Cascading Ivy cake.

 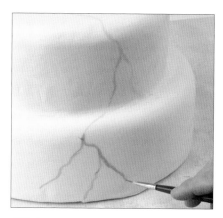 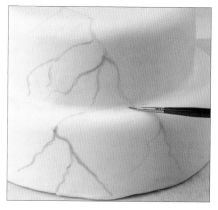

4 Mix a little food grade alcohol with mid green edible dusting powder to make a small amount of green paint.

5 Use a size 1 round brush to draw a fine trailing line of green paint down the side of the cake.

6 The alcohol will gradually evaporate as you work, so make another small amount of paint if necessary. Extend the trailing lines.

7 Put a size 2 round nozzle into an icing bag and fill it with royal icing. Use this to attach the lighter ivy leaves.

8 Build up the design with more ivy leaves, making a few at a time so that they remain flexible. Vary the tones by introducing mid green and autumn green when colouring them, and overlay the lighter leaves with these more muted tones.

Opposite

Details from the finished Cascading Ivy cake.

72

ALPHABET BLOCKS

This project uses very simple stencilling for very effective results. The dusting technique is used to tint white icing with letters, which are then cut out with a mini cupcake cutter before being applied to the prepared cake. Perfect for a christening or baby shower cake, the same techniques can be used for a child's birthday cake.

You will need

Letter alphabet stencils
1 or more 5cm (2in) cube cakes, covered in pink sugarpaste
White sugarpaste
15mm (⅝in) flat brush
Edible dusting powder in pearlescent pink
5cm (2in) circle cutter
Palette knife
White vegetable fat
Edible glue

1 Cut a 5cm (2in) sponge cake into a cube and cover it with pink sugarpaste.

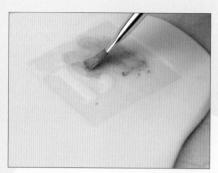

2 Follow the instructions for dusting on page 21 with white sugarpaste, the letter B stencil, a 15mm (⅝in) flat brush and pearlescent pink powder.

3 Repeat the process until you have completed five copies of the letter block. Cut out each copy with the 5cm (2in) circle cutter.

4 Use the palette knife to carefully lift one of the letter blocks on to the top of the cake.

5 Place the circle cutter over the top of the letter block and gently rotate it around the letter block to ensure the piece is perfectly circular.

6 Use edible glue to attach a letter block to each of the sides of the cake.

Opposite

The finished Alphabet Blocks cake, along with two others prepared using the same techniques.

TOWER OF CUPCAKES

This project shows how simple stencilling on to plain icing can be transformed by creating depth and dimension. The vibrant colours against white icing create fantastic results.

You will need

Mini Quilting stencil
1 or more cupcakes
White sugarpaste
Small rolling pin
15mm (⅝in) flat brush
Edible dusting powder
in purple
2cm (¾in) circle cutter
Leaf cutter
Palette knife
Smoothing tool
White vegetable fat

1 Knead a small amount of white sugarpaste and roll it out to 2mm (¹⁄₁₆in) thick using a small rolling pin. Place the stencil on top and use a 15mm (⅝in) flat brush to dust the whole area with purple dusting powder.

2 Remove the stencil then use the 2cm (¾in) circle cutter to cut out as many circles as possible from the area. You will need seven for each cupcake.

3 Carefully clear away the excess icing, using a small kitchen knife to help in tight areas.

4 Pick up one of the circles on the end of your palette knife and gently roll it up, with the leading edge slightly open as shown.

5 Pick up a second circle on your palette knife and place the rolled-up piece on top. Gently pinch the bottoms of the pieces together.

6 Pick up a third circle and roll it around the second, overlapping one side of the second piece as shown.

7 Wrap another four circles around in the same way, gradually building up the petals of the flower. Let the outer petals leading edges fall away slightly for a more open flower.

8 Use the palette knife to carefully trim away the bottom to leave a flat base.

The finished Tower of Cupcakes.

9 Ice a cupcake with sugarpaste and place the flower on top. Secure it with a dab of water or edible glue.

10 Roll out another small piece of sugarpaste to a thickness of 4mm (⅛in) using a small rolling pin. Place the stencil on top and use a 15mm (⅝in) flat brush to dust the whole stencil area with purple dusting powder.

11 Place the leaf cutter on to the icing and press it down, then lift it away.

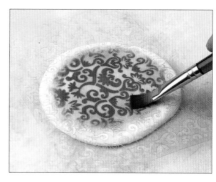

12 Make two leaves for each cupcake and attach them to the cupcake with a little water, tucking them underneath the petals of the flower.

13 Make as many cupcakes with flowers as you need.

14 Roll white sugarpaste out to a thickness of 6mm (¼in) using a small rolling pin. Place the stencil on top and use a 15mm (⅝in) flat brush to dust the whole stencil area with purple dusting powder.

15 Remove the stencil, then use a circle cutter slightly larger than your cupcake to cut out a circle. Pick it up on your palette knife and place it on top of your cupcake.

16 Use the smoothing tool to round the edges of the circle slightly, then decorate as many cupcakes as you need in the same way.

Opposite
Details of the Tower of Cupcakes.

INDEX